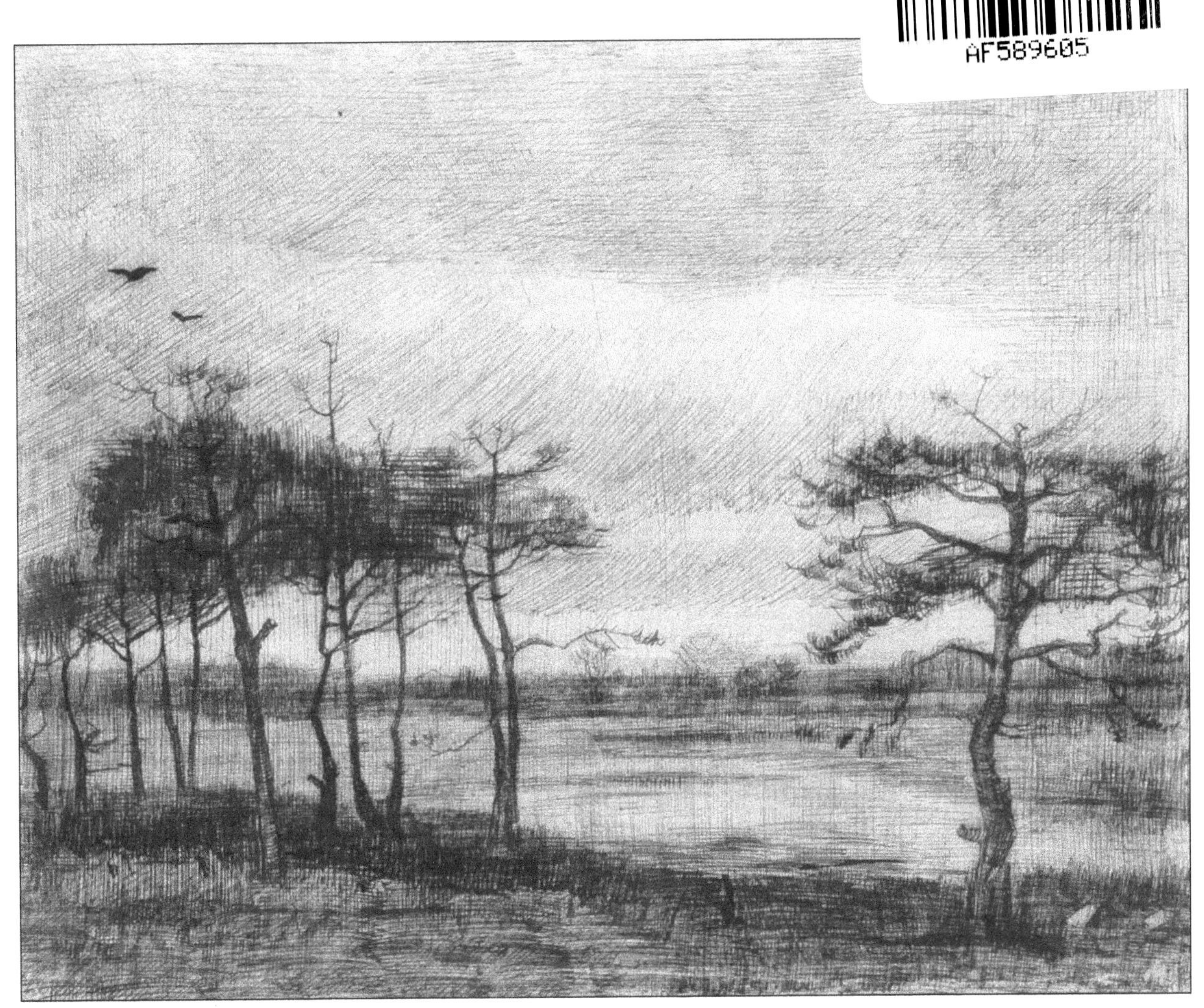

"Drawing is the root of everything."
— Vincent Van Gogh

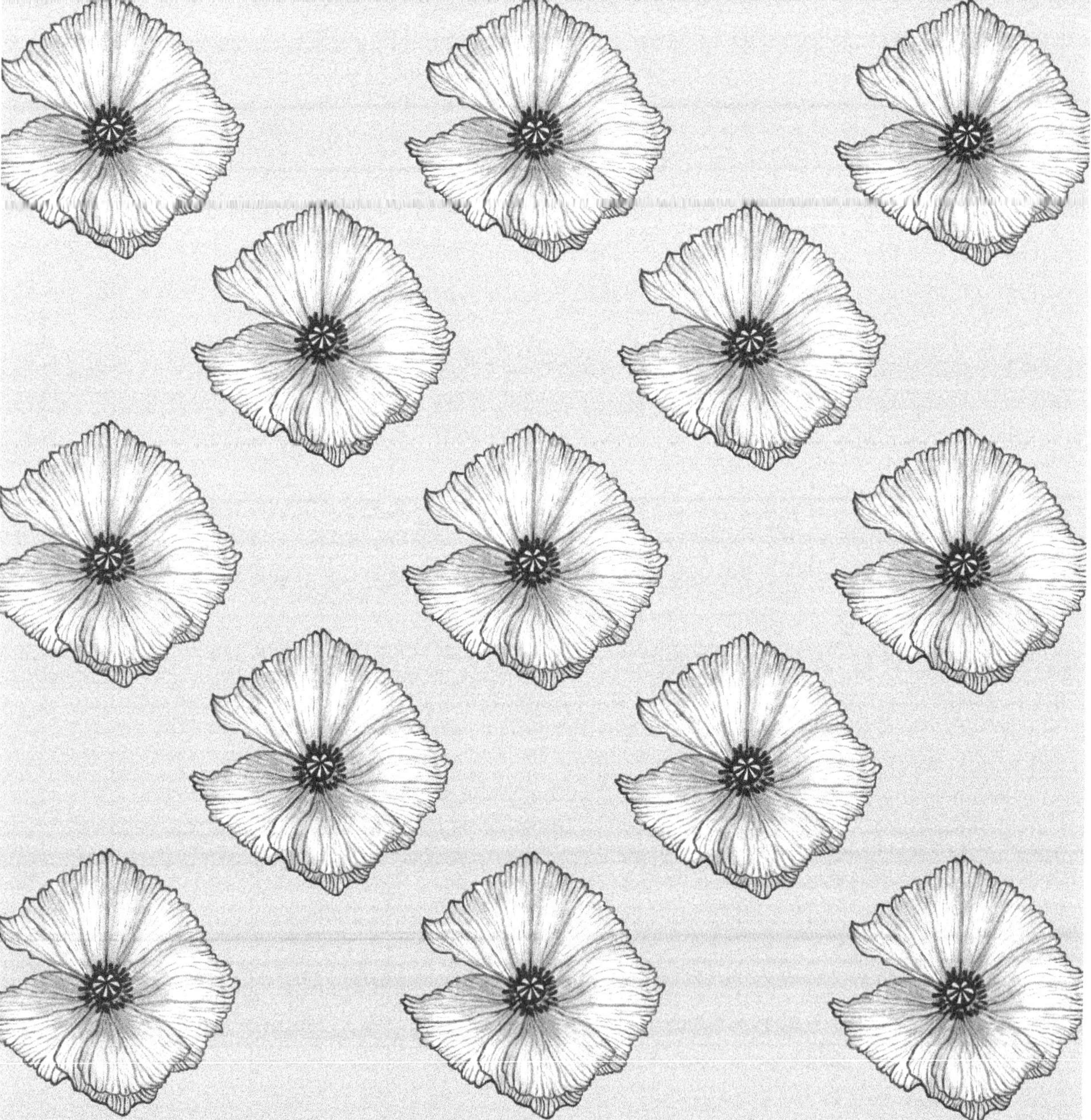

How to See Like an Artist!

SKETCHBOOK

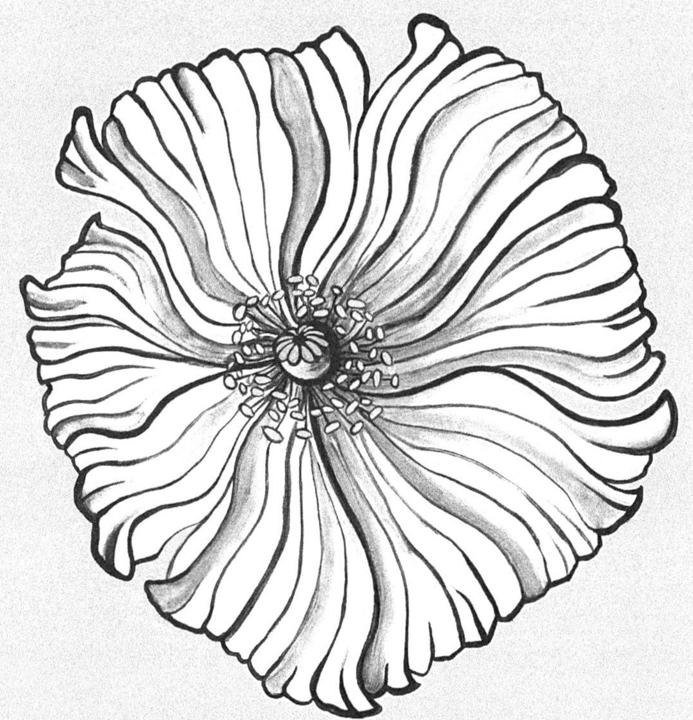

Ariane Trifunovic Montemuro

Ideas into Books: Westview
Kingston Springs, Tennessee

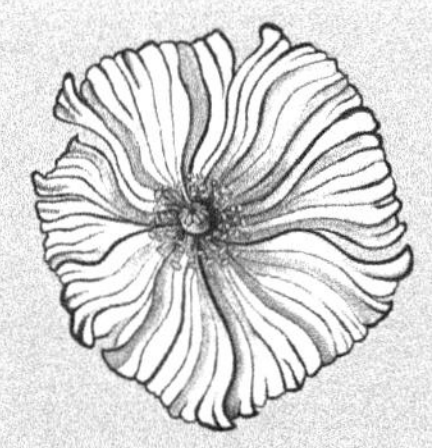

Ideas into Books®
W E S T V I E W
P.O. Box 605
Kingston Springs, TN 37082
www.publishedbywestview.com

Cover Graphic Design
Jeri Wofford

Interior Book Graphic Design
Elaine P. Millen, TeknoLink Marketing Services, www.teknolinkmarketingservices.com

Photo Credits
Documented at the end of the book

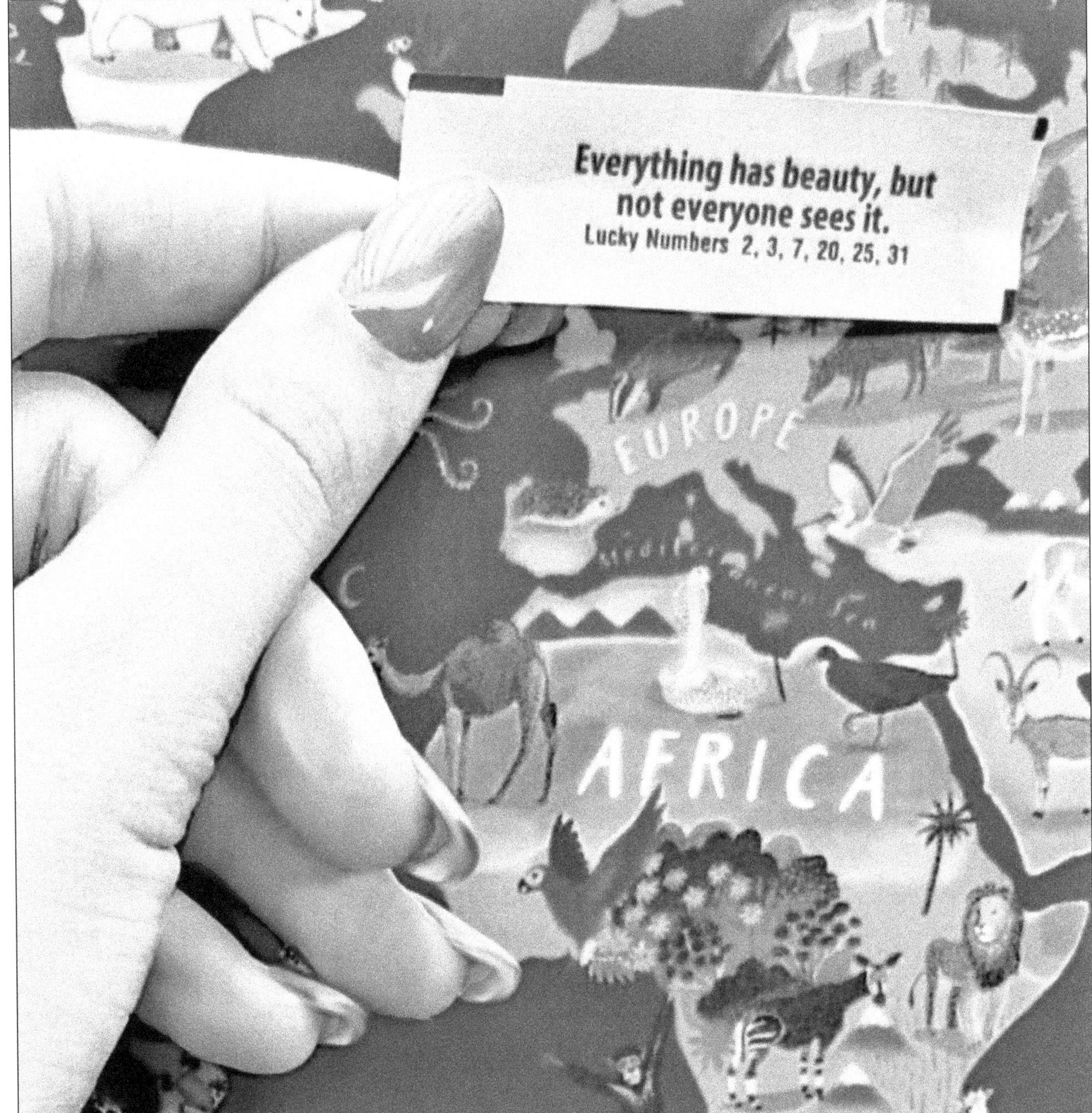
Everything has beauty, but
not everyone sees it.
Lucky Numbers 2, 3, 7, 20, 25, 31
EUROPE
AFRICA

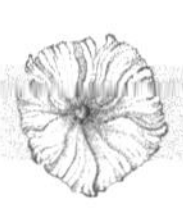

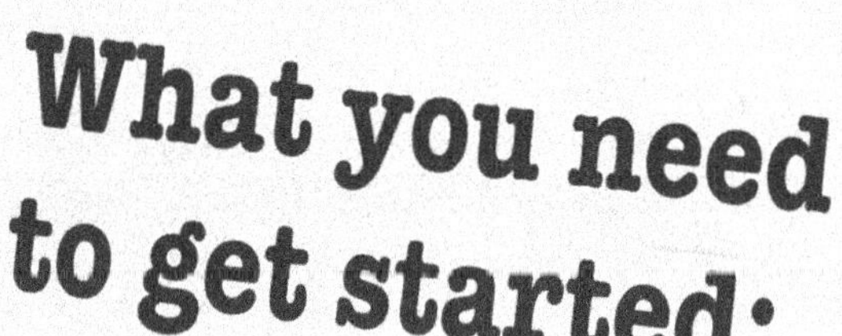

- A pencil for drawing
- A set of colored pencils
- An eraser

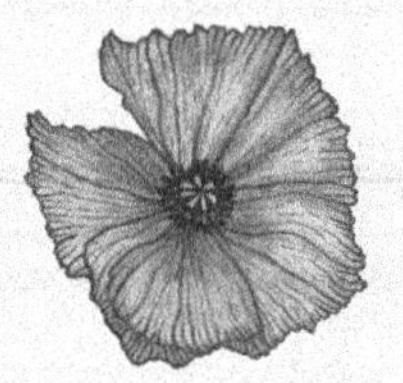

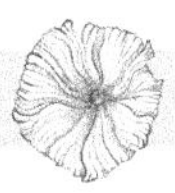

SKETCHBOOK TIPS

Ready. Set. Go! It's time to See Like an Artist.

Each of us possesses a special way of seeing and noticing things others might not. Our field of view is uniquely our own. We just have to be courageous and express it.

Look around your world. Notice what inspires and delights your eyes. Start with the basics. Study the variety of *lines* you encounter. Some are short, long, thin, thick, straight, zig zag – just to name a few! Next up, look for *shapes*. When a line catches its tail, it forms a shape. After that look for color. Colors can be warm like the sun and cool like water. Delve deeper into looking for a variety of subjects to draw and color. Study and draw the visual and tactile surface character or *texture* of things you see like smooth glass and rough tree bark. Study and draw shadows around objects. A shadow places a form firmly in its spot. When you draw, change the layout of your objects and try forming new compositional arrangements. Make it a practice to draw the same thing again and again. Don't forget to copy the artwork of Old Masters. This practice of copying is invaluable to develop your skills as an artist! Do you have a few favorite artists? If not, open a book on art history and find some. An artist you admire can inspire you in your work.

Observe and keep drawing everyday things every day. Always remember that drawing is a skill anyone can learn, develop and refine. The key is to pick up your pencil, study your subject carefully, and draw. *You know the saying, use it or lose it!*

Its time to grab inspiration from everything you see. After all, that's what artists do!

Here are composition vocabulary words to reflect upon as you begin to express your vision.

- **Shape and proportion**
- **Positioning**
- **Cropping**
- **Negative space**
- **Color**
- **Contrast: the value, or degree of lightness and darkness, used within the picture**
- **Lines**
- **Lighting**
- **Repetition**
- **Perspective**
- **Harmony or disharmony between objects used to express a thought**
- **Blurred or busy background**
- **Emphasis**

It's important to incorporate these principles of organization in your art. They will help you depict what you are trying to say with your work. **Compare them to a recipe, and use these ingredients to help organize your composition.**

Use the following blank pages for sketching your ideas. ▶

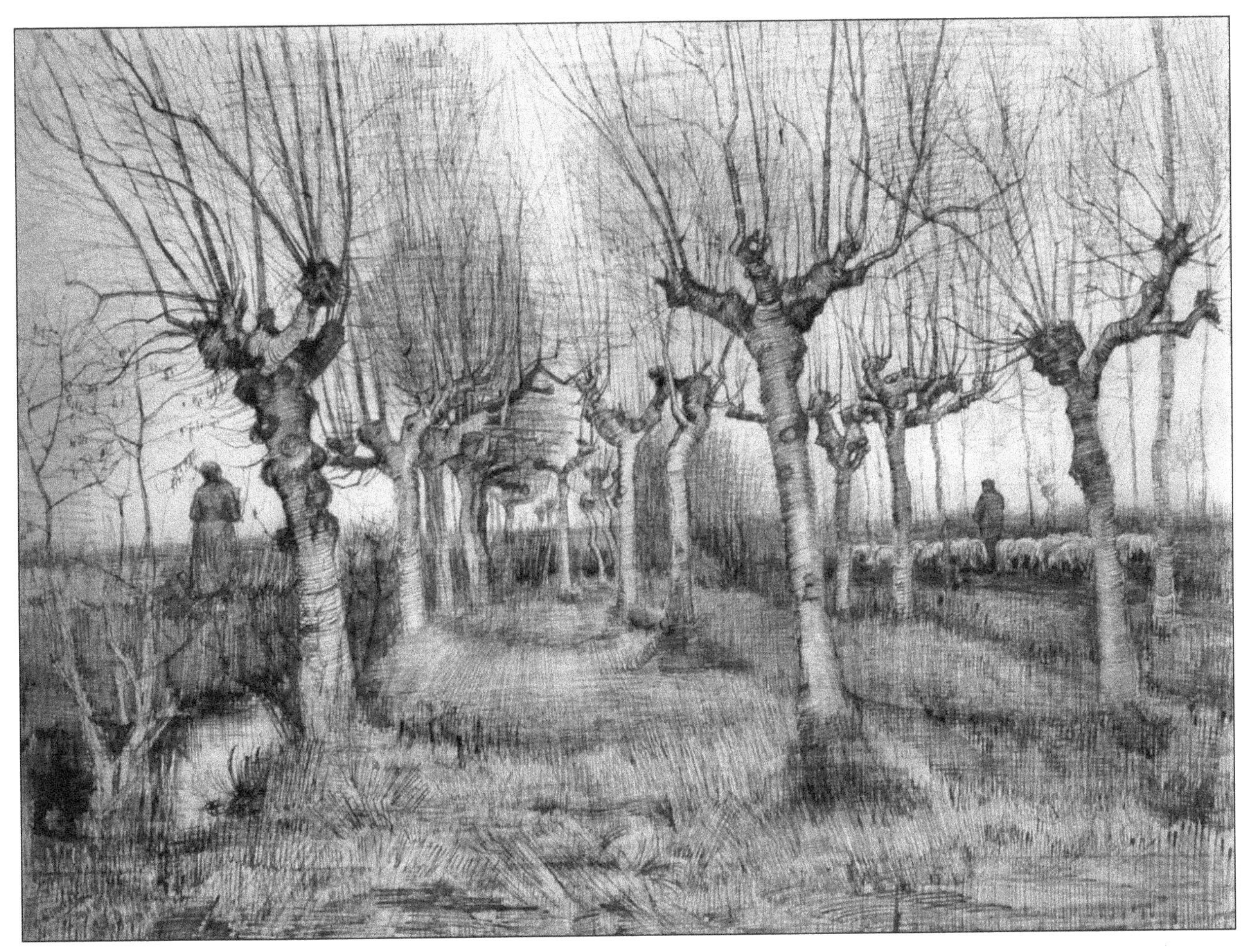

"Find things beautiful as much as you can,
most people find too little beautiful."

— Vincent Van Gogh

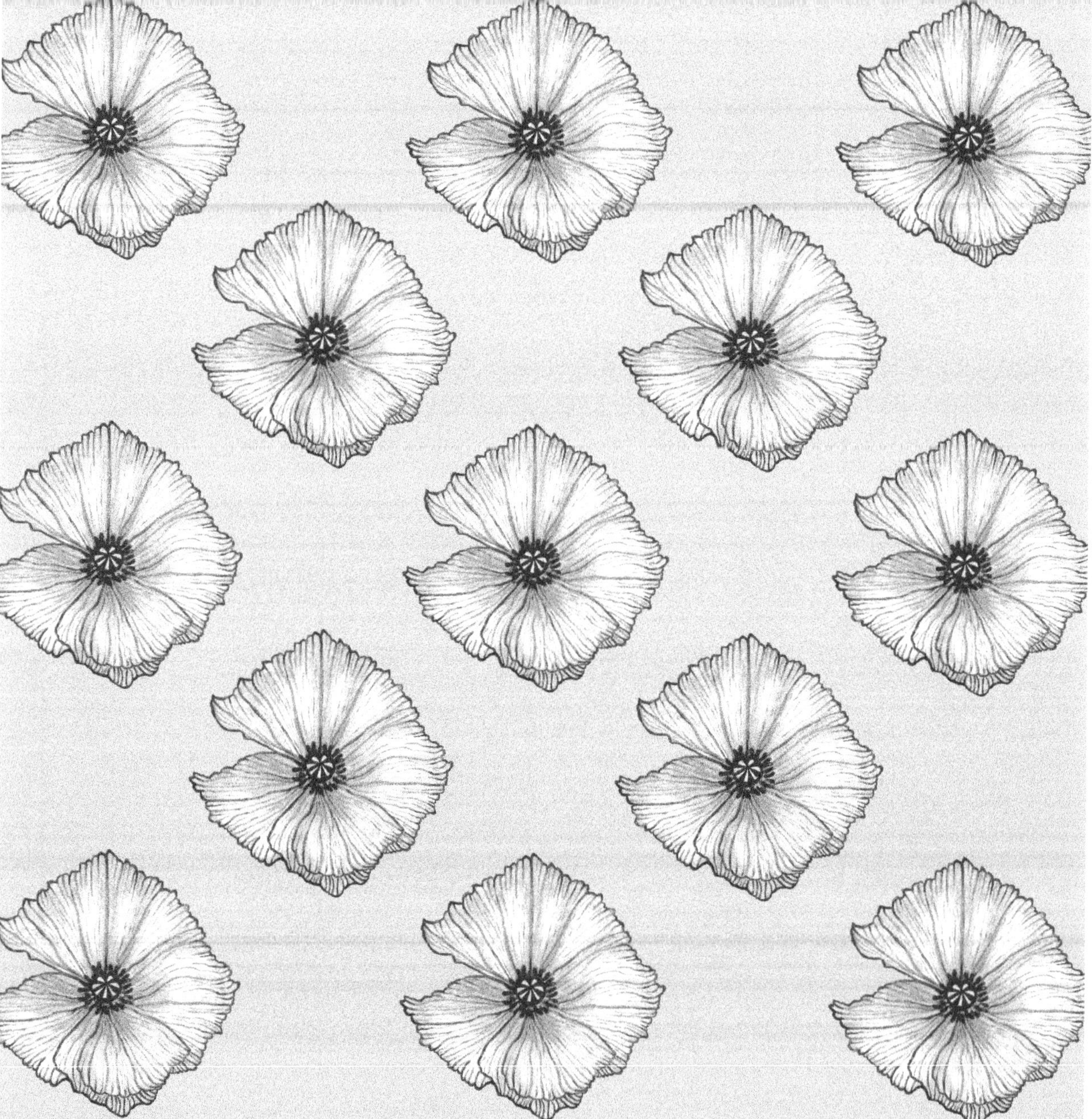

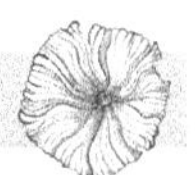

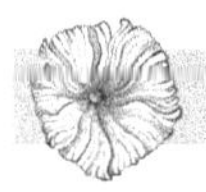

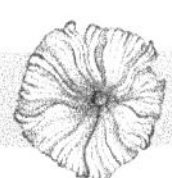

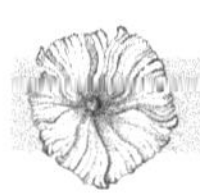

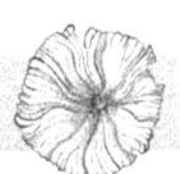

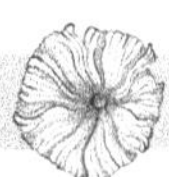

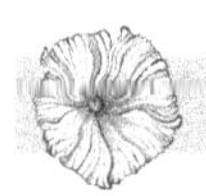

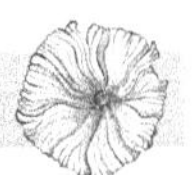

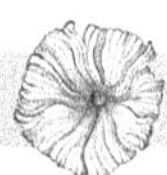

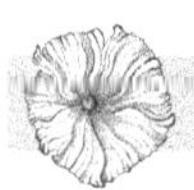

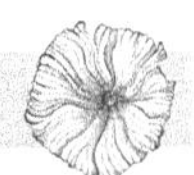

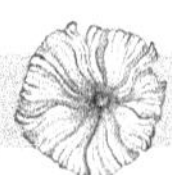

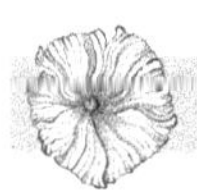

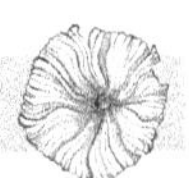

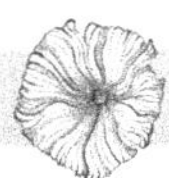

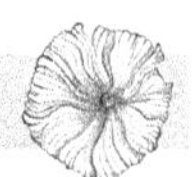

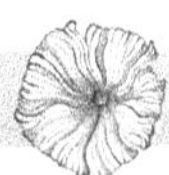

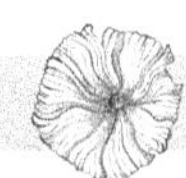

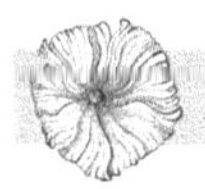

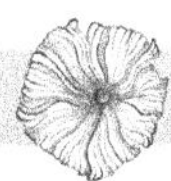

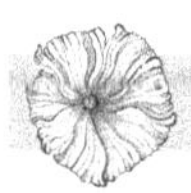

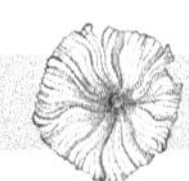

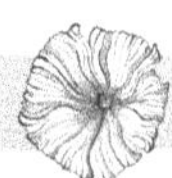

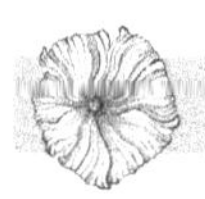

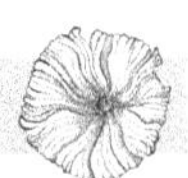

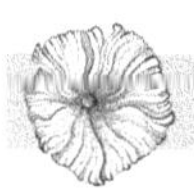

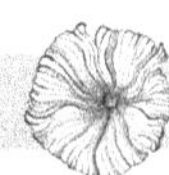

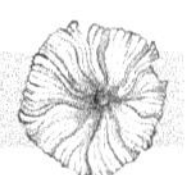

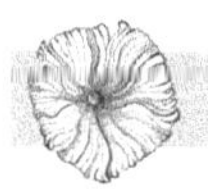

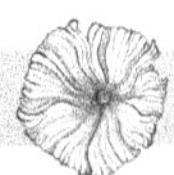

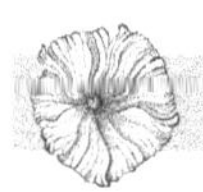

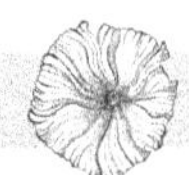

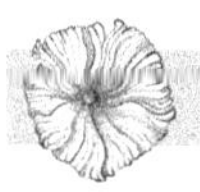

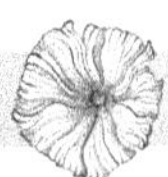

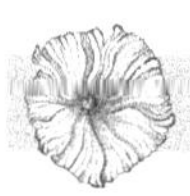

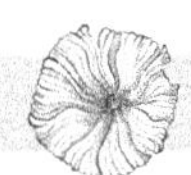

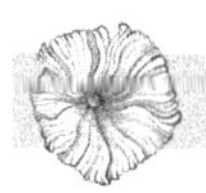

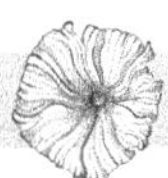

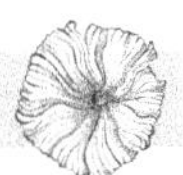

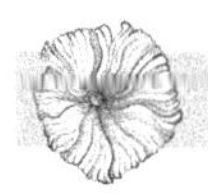

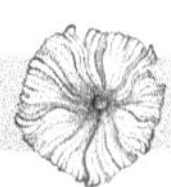

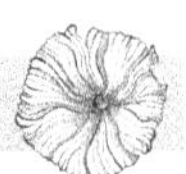

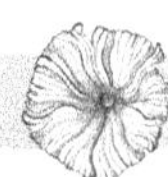

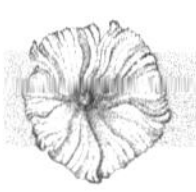

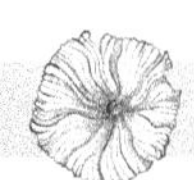

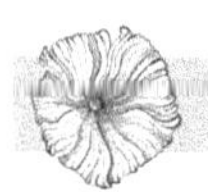

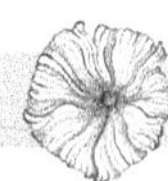

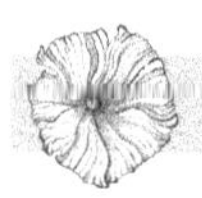

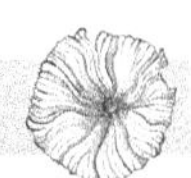

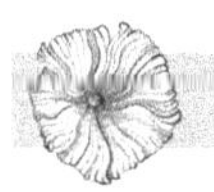

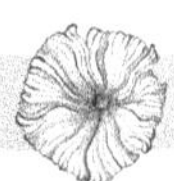

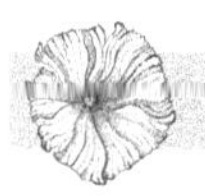

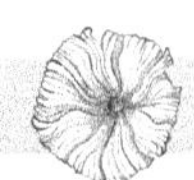

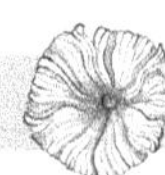

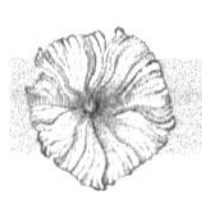

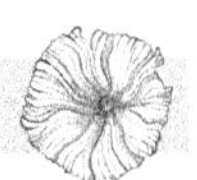

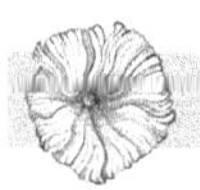

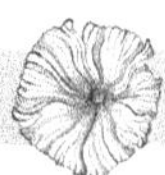

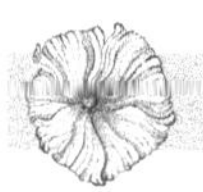

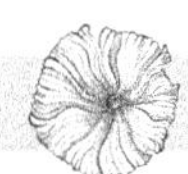

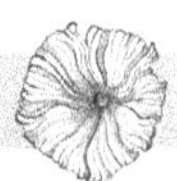

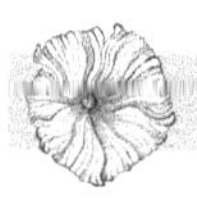

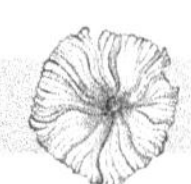

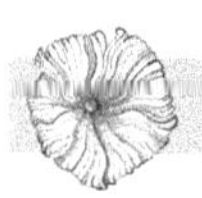

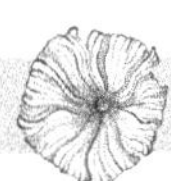

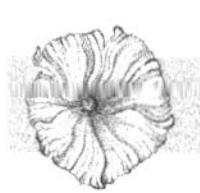

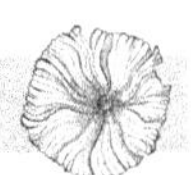

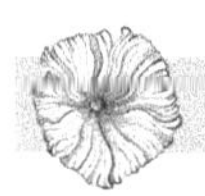

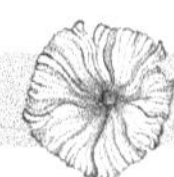

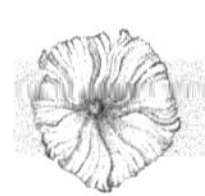

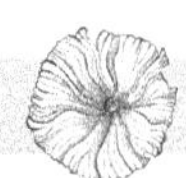

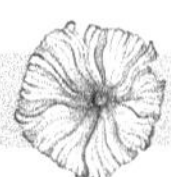

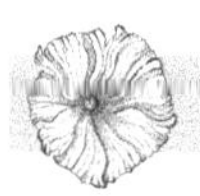

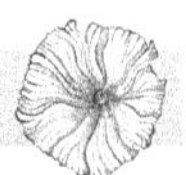

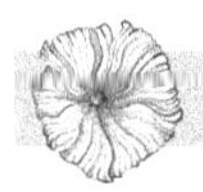

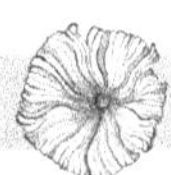

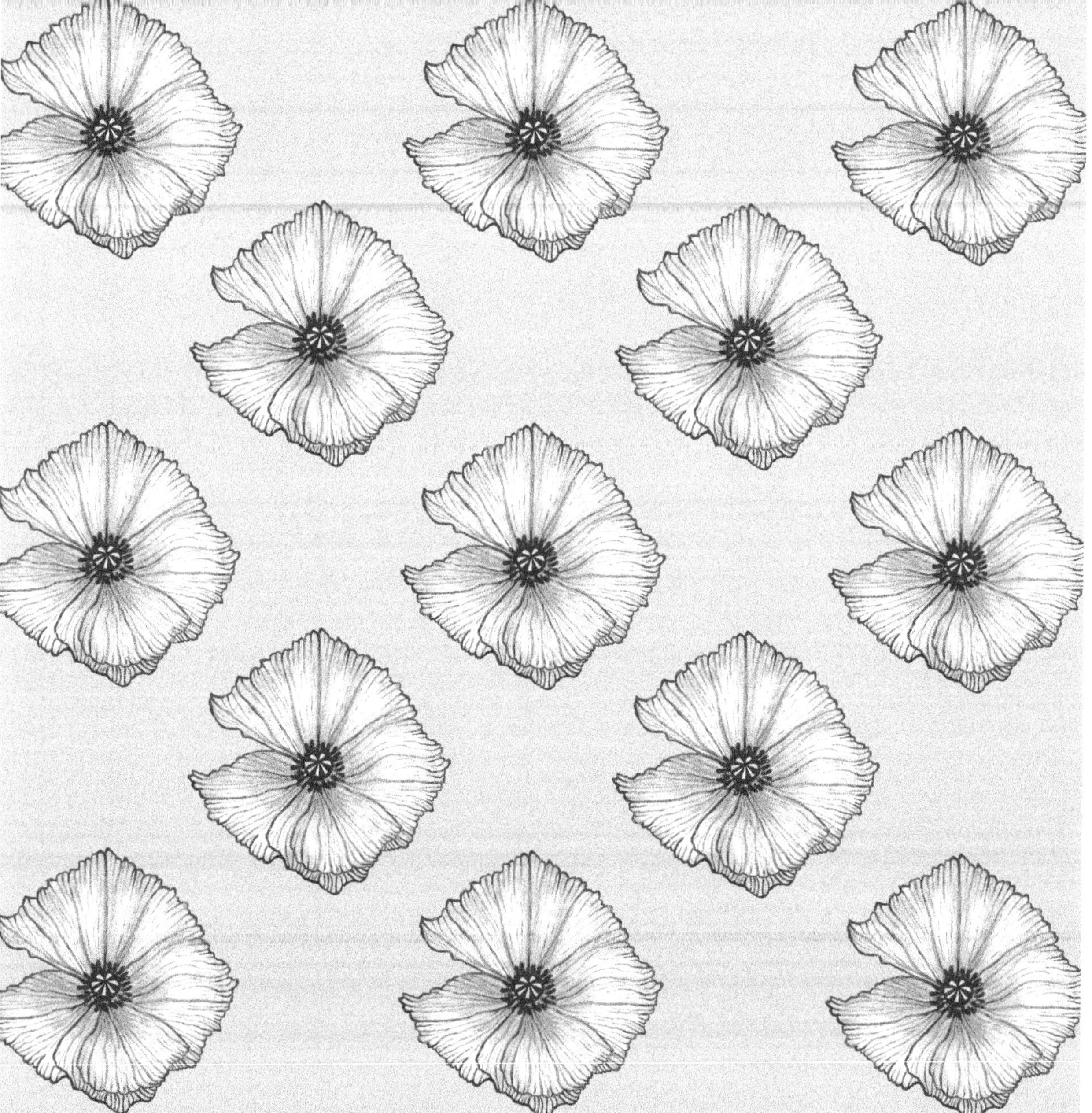

How to See Like an Artist!

SKETCHBOOK

PHOTO CREDITS

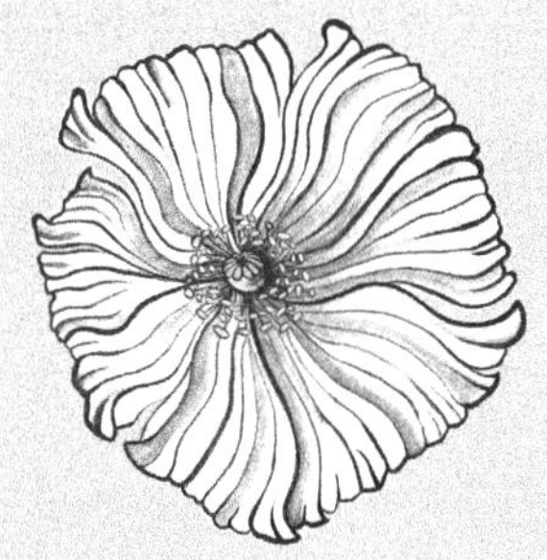

Photo Credits

All images used in this book were created by or for Ariane Trifunovic Montemuro except for the ones that are listed below. Those come from a variety of resources including but not limited to public domain, Creative Commons, stock photography, and others.

Dancer Adjusting Her Slipper
Edgar Degas
1873
H.L. Havemeyer Collection,
Bequest of Mrs. H.O. Havermeyer, 1929
The Met
Public Domain

Ideal Head of a Woman
Michelangelo
1525
Wikimedia Commons
Public Domain

Impression, Sunrise
Claude Monet
1872
Musée Marmottan Monet, Paris, France
Public Domain

Pencils
www.unsplash.com

Pine Trees in the Fen
Vincent van Gogh
1884
WikiArt Visual Art Encyclopedia
Public Domain

Poppies, Isles of Shoals
1891
Childe Hassam
National Gallery of Art
Gift of Margaret and Raymond Horowitz
Public Domain

Poppy Field in Giverny
Claude Monet
1890
WikiArt Visual Art Encyclopedia
Public Domain

Pollard Birches
Vincent van Gogh
1884
WikiArt Visual Art Encyclopedia
Public Domain

Portrait of Juan Gris
Amedeo Mondigliani
1915
Wikimedia Commons
Public Domain

The Singer in Green
Edgar Degas
1884
Bequest of Stephen C. Clark, 1960
The Met
Public Domain

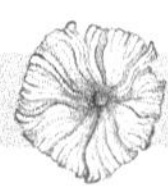

The Starry Night
Vincent van Gogh
1889
Museum of Modern Art Collection
Google Art Project
Wikipedia
Public Domain

Sun Giorgio Maggiore at Dusk
Claude Monet
1908-1912
Bequeath of Gwendoline Davies
National Museum Cardiff, Cardiff, Wales
Wikimedia Commons
Public Domain

Young Woman with Ibis
Edgar Degas
1857-58/Reworked 1860-62
Gift of Stephen Mazoh and Purchase,
Bequest of Gioconda King, by exchange, 2008
The Met
Public Domain

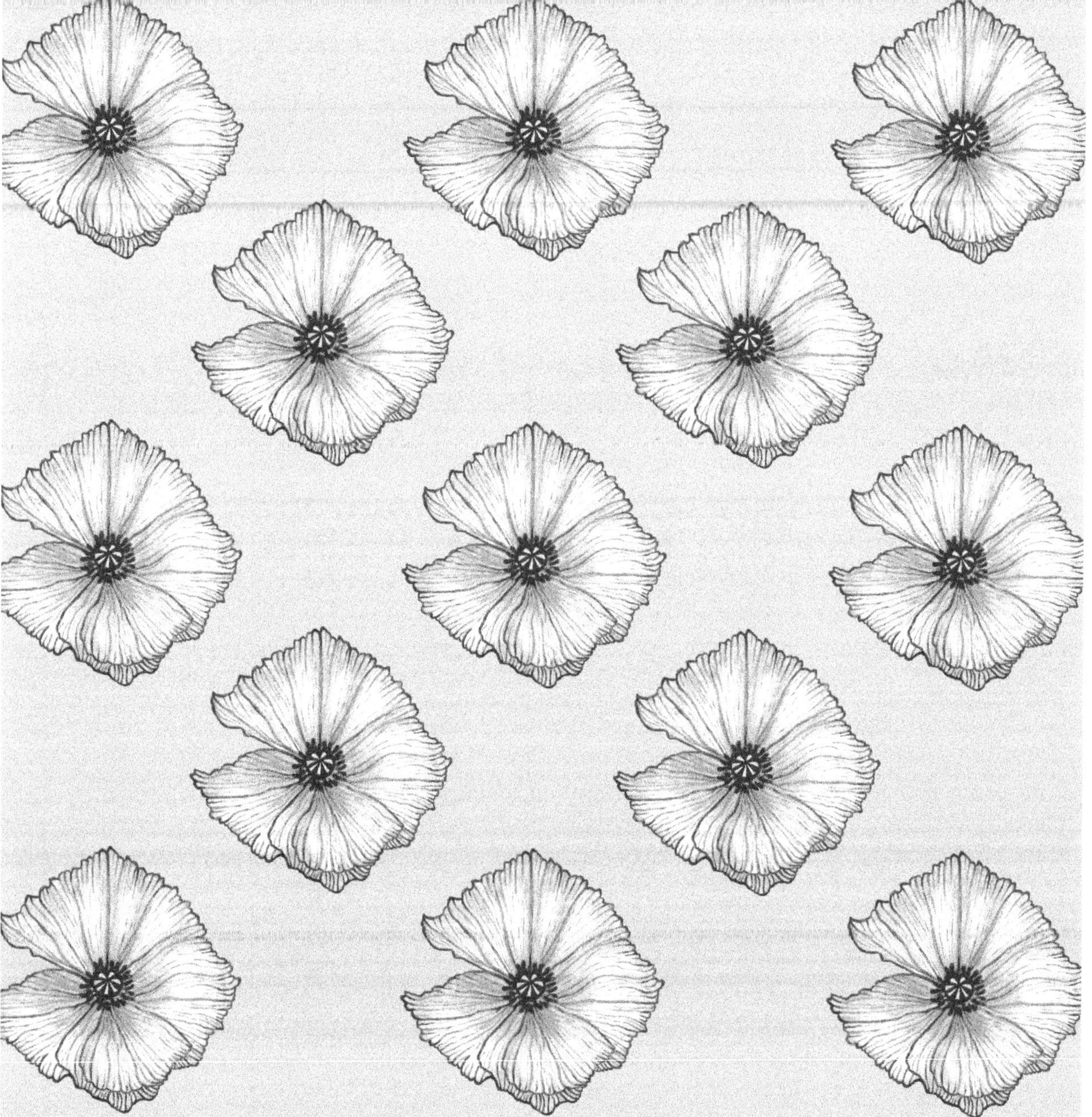

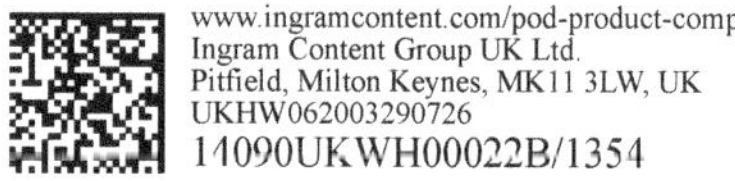
www.ingramcontent.com/pod-product-compliance
Ingram Content Group UK Ltd.
Pitfield, Milton Keynes, MK11 3LW, UK
UKHW062003290726
14090UKWH00022B/1354